The Library of SPIDERS™

Funnel Weavers

JAKE MILLER

The Rosen Publishing Group's
PowerKids Press™
New York

Published in 2004 by The Rosen Publishing Group, Inc.
29 East 21st Street, New York, NY 10010

First Edition

Editor: Jannell Khu
Book Design: Emily Muschinske
Layout Design: Eric DePalo
Photo Research: Emily Muschinske

Photo Credits:Cover and pp. 1, 5, 10, 13, 14 © Robert and Linda Mitchell;
pp. 6, 9, 10 (inset), 14, 17, 18 © Ed Nieuwenhuys; p. 21 © Pan Photo/Peter Kubal.

Miller, Jake, 1969–
  Funnel weavers / Jake Miller.
    p. cm. — (The library of spiders)
  Includes bibliographical references and index.
  Contents: Funnel weavers — The agelenidae family — The funnel weaver's body — Spinning silk — The funnel web — How funnel
weavers hunt — Funnel weaver's eggs — Baby funnel weavers — A funnel weaver's enemies — Funnel weaver's relationship with people.
  ISBN 0-8239-6709-3 (lib. bdg.)
  1. Agelenidae—Juvenile literature.   [1. Funnel-web spiders. 2. Spiders.]   I. Title. II. Series.
QL458.42.A3M55 2004
595.4'4—dc21

2002012664

Manufactured in the United States of America

Contents

Funnel Weavers

Early on summer mornings, many grass fields are scattered with thin tangled sheets of spiderwebs. Dewdrops make these spiderwebs sparkle. Many of these webs are the work of grass spiders, which belong to a group of spiders called funnel weavers. Funnel weavers spin sheetlike webs that spread out into the grass with an opening that is narrow and funnel shaped. These spiders can range in size from about ⅓ to ¾ inch (8–19 mm). Most funnel weavers are harmless to humans.

Inside the narrow, funnel-shaped opening is where the spiders rest, hide from danger, and wait to attack insects that become trapped in the web's messy threads.

4

The Agelenidae Family

Funnel weavers are members of the **Agelenidae family**. There are about 700 known **species** of Agelenidae. They live throughout the world, in many different **habitats**. Most Agelenidae live by themselves in small webs that they make in fields. A few species in the African jungles live together in big groups. They share their webs. Funnel weavers also live in deserts, woods, and houses. Each kind of Agelenidae looks different, and each has a specific way of life. Even members of the same species may develop different behaviors in order to **survive**. Grass spiders that live in one habitat may develop a hunting style that is different from the hunting style of grass spiders that live in another habitat. Spiders living in the desert are more **aggressive** than spiders living in a forest or near a stream.

These spiders belong to the Agelenidae family. There are about 400 different species of Agelenidae in North America.

The Funnel Weaver's Body

All funnel weaver species have some things in common with one another. They have light hairs on their bodies. Their eight long, slender legs are covered with bristles. Many funnel weaver species have eight eyes as do most spiders. All spiders have two main parts to their bodies. The head, or **cephalothorax**, is the front part of the body, to which the legs are attached. The rear part of the body is called the **abdomen**. The abdomen contains the spider's **silk glands**, which make the silk used to spin the web.

All true spiders have two main body parts, the cephalothorax and the abdomen. The spider shown on the opposite page belongs to the Agelenidae family.

8

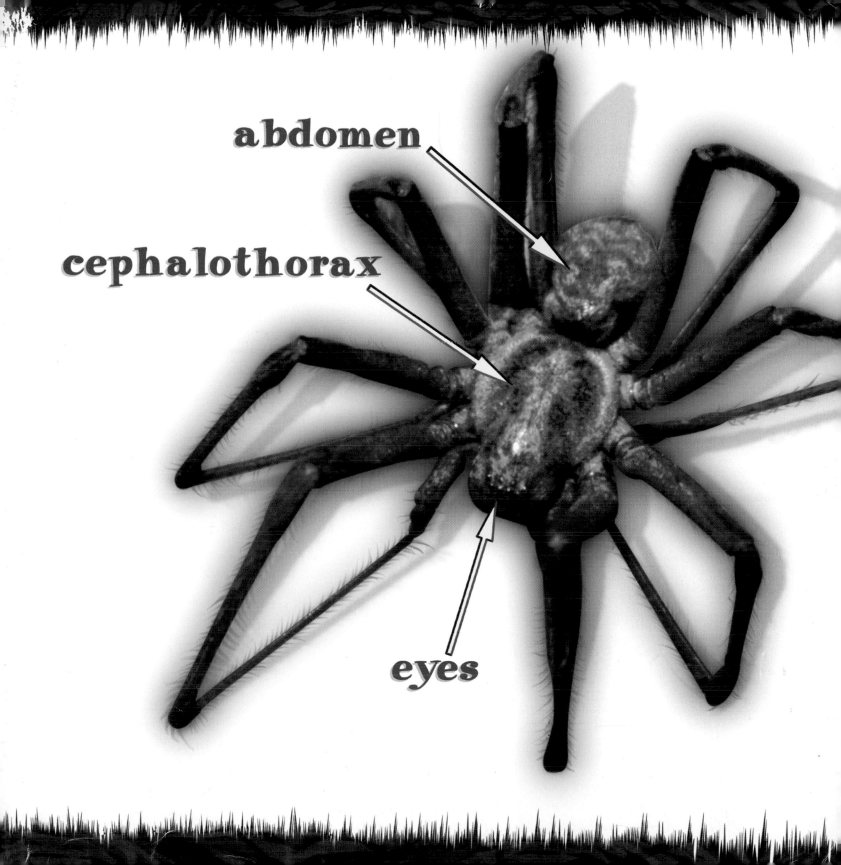

abdomen

cephalothorax

eyes

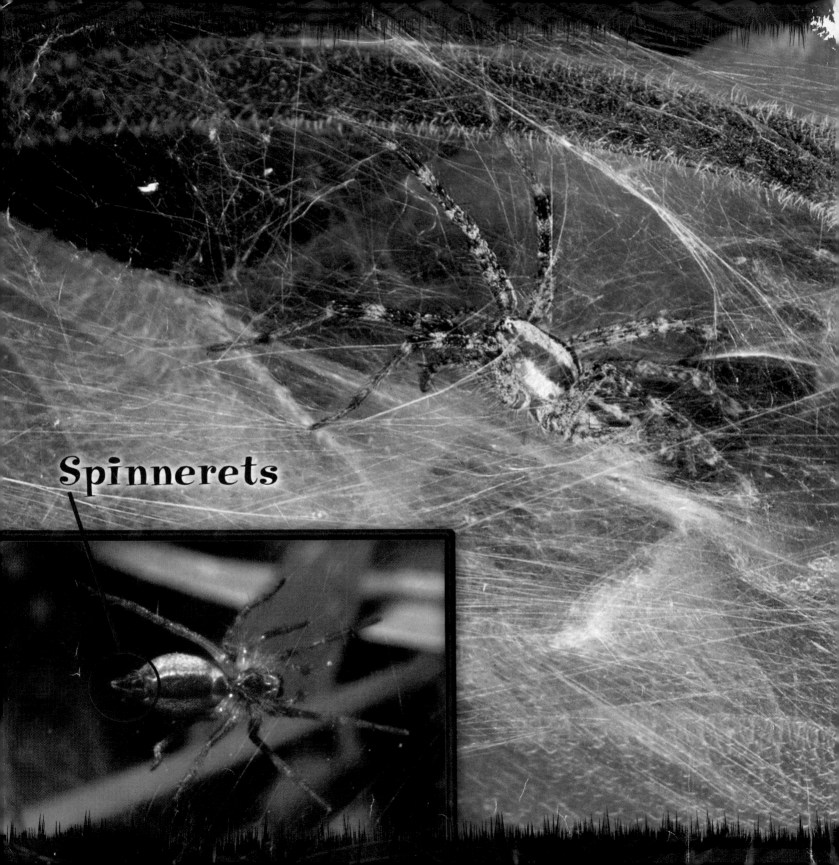

Spinnerets

Spinning Silk

Spiders use their **spinnerets** to weave the silk for their webs. The spinnerets look like little tubes that stick out of the spider's body. Funnel weavers have two pairs of spinnerets. They have a short pair toward the front of the abdomen and a longer pair that stick out of the back tip of the abdomen. The spinnerets are **adapted** to make the kind of silk that funnel weavers use to make their special webs. It takes a funnel weaver about two hours to make a new web. The spider uses the energy from two days' worth of feeding to make the web! Some kinds of spiders, such as orb weavers, make a new web every night, but Agelenidae webs are more **permanent**. Instead of making new webs, they fix holes and make the webs they already have bigger.

These funnel weavers are spinning webs in the grass. The silk comes out of their spinnerets. As a funnel weaver grows, it adds new layers to its web to make it bigger.

The Funnel Web

Agelenidae spin a funnel-shaped **retreat** at one end of their web. This is where they hide from their enemies and from the insects that they hunt for food. Funnel weavers build their webs between blades of grass, in spaces under rocks, in piles of fallen leaves, and over branches and bushes. The web is a trap for the funnel weaver's **prey**. The messy threads of a funnel weaver's web are not sticky. However, the tangled web slows down prey and confuses it. This gives the funnel weaver a chance to catch prey!

Funnel weavers add to their webs every day. A grass spider's web may get as large as 1 square yard (.8 sq m). The web's funnel can be up to 1 foot (30 cm) deep.

How Funnel Weavers Hunt

Agelenidae spend most of their time out of sight, in the funnel at the end of the web. The web is not only a trap for prey but also a kind of alarm system for the spider. When something lands on the web, the spider can feel the web move as the **intruder** tries to walk across it. The funnel weaver can then dash out of its funnel for a surprise attack.

Funnel weavers can move very fast. As quickly as they can, they run out and bite their prey. The **venom** in their bite **paralyzes** prey. When the prey is paralyzed, the funnel weavers drag their victims into their funnel, where they can eat in safety. Funnel weavers eat moths, grasshoppers, beetles, butterflies, and other insects.

(Top) This funnel weaver hides inside its funnel-shaped retreat and patiently waits to trap prey. (Bottom) If you want to see a funnel weaver's web, it is best to get up early on a summer morning. Morning dewdrops cling to this funnel weaver's web.

A Funnel Weaver's Eggs

The male funnel weaver leaves his web to search for a female when it is time to **mate**. He signals to her by stroking her web. She senses his movement and lets him onto her web, where they mate. A female lays from 100 to 200 eggs. Then she builds a protective egg sac from silk. She places the egg sac on a rock, covers it with dead leaves, and then adds a layer of loosely woven silk. Eggs of species that live in warm areas hatch about one month after they are laid. In cold areas, females lay eggs in October. The eggs hatch in the spring.

Not all of these baby funnel weavers will live. Some will be eaten by insects.

Baby Funnel Weavers

A day or so after they hatch, baby funnel weavers, or spiderlings, climb to a high, windy place and spin a single strand of silk. The wind catches the silk strands and carries the spiderlings away. It is as if the spiderlings are flying on hang gliders or balloons. This is called ballooning.

When a spiderling lands in a new spot, it starts its own web. Unfortunately, many of the flying baby spiders land in places where they will quickly die. For instance, they may land in the middle of a lake, or in a parking lot where they may get stepped on by people. This is one of the reasons that a female funnel weaver lays so many eggs. If she lays a lot of eggs, at least a few of the hundreds of spiderlings will survive.

These spiderlings are walking on the web that their mother has made. Soon they will leave by ballooning and make their own funnel webs.

Funnel Weavers' Enemies

Funnel weavers have many enemies. Birds, lizards, insects such as praying mantises, and other spiders all prey on Agelenidae. A funnel weaver's best **defense** is the funnel in its web. The spider tries to build its web so that the funnel leads to a safe place where the spider can go to escape danger. The funnel often leads into a crack between two rocks or into thick plants, where the spider's enemies can't follow. Spiders will only bite their enemies in self-defense, when they can't escape any other way.

The praying mantis is one of the funnel weaver's many enemies. Funnel weavers that live inside people's houses may even be attacked by pet cats!

Spider Bites

Spiders and their webs can have medical benefits. People once used spider webs as bandages. Today, scientists study the venom of funnel weavers to see how it can be used in drugs to fight illnesses such as Alzheimer's disease.

Funnel Weavers and People

Most funnel weavers are harmless to humans. Some people are **allergic** to spider bites. The venom of a few Agelenidae species, such as the **hobo** spider, is dangerous to people. The wound from a hobo spider's bite forms a blister, which then turns into a black scab that may take months to heal. The bite can also cause headaches and weakness. These problems may last up to one week. People who think that they have been bitten by a hobo spider should see a doctor as soon as they can. You can help to avoid the spider bites by wearing long sleeves and gloves when working in the grass or around firewood piles.

For the most part, however, funnel weavers are good to have around. Their webs are beautiful on summer mornings, and they eat many insects that can be annoying or dangerous to humans and to crops.

Glossary

abdomen (AB-duh-min) The large, rear section of an insect's or a spider's body.

adapted (uh-DAPT-id) To have changed to fit new conditions.

Agelenidae (a-juh-LEH-nih-dee) The family of spiders to which funnel weavers belong.

aggressive (uh-GREH-siv) Ready to fight.

allergic (uh-LER-jik) Getting a little sick from something.

cephalothorax (sef-uh-loh-THOR-aks) A spider's smaller, front body part, containing its head.

defense (DEE-fents) Something that guards from harm.

family (FAM-lee) The scientific name for a large group of plants or animals that are alike in some ways.

habitats (HA-bih-tats) Surroundings where an animal or a plant naturally lives.

hobo (HOH-boh) A person who travels around a lot, often by riding on trains.

intruder (in-TROOD-er) Something that goes into a place without being invited.

mate (MAYT) To join together to make babies.

paralyzes (PAR-uh-lyz-iz) Causes to lose feeling or movement in the limbs.

permanent (PER-muh-nint) Lasting forever.

prey (PRAY) An animal that is hunted by another animal for food.

retreat (ree-TREET) A safe place to hide or get away.

silk glands (SILK GLANDZ) Body parts of a spider that produce silk.

species (SPEE-sheez) A single kind of plant or animal. All people are one species.

spinnerets (spih-nuh-RETS) Body parts, located on the rear of the spider's abdomen, that release silk.

survive (sur-VYV) To live longer than; to stay alive.

venom (VEH-num) A poison passed by one animal into another through a bite or a sting.

Index

Web Sites

Due to the changing nature of Internet links, PowerKids Press has developed an online list of Web sites related to the subject of this book. This site is updated regularly. Please use this link to access the list:
www.powerkidslinks.com/lspi/funnel/